SESAME STREET®

Celebrating YOU and ME

T0011929

Many Ways to
BELIEVE

Christy Peterson

Lerner Publications ◆ Minneapolis

On Sesame Street, we celebrate everyone!

In this series, readers will explore the different ways we eat, dress, play, and more. Recognizing our similarities and differences will teach little ones to be proud of themselves and appreciate the world around them. Together, we can all be smarter, stronger, and kinder.

Sincerely, the Editors at Sesame Workshop

Table of Contents

Respecting Beliefs

Many people
follow a religion,
or a set of beliefs.

Learning more about religions helps me respect others.

All about Religions

Some people have a place where they come together to practice their religion.

Some people gather in a church, a temple, or a mosque.

Sometimes that place is outside.

7

Some people wear special clothes for their religion. Some people wear a covering over their head or hair such as patkas, kippahs, or hijabs.

There are all kinds of head coverings! Elmo thinks they're all special.

9

A lot of religions celebrate holidays. Families and friends gather to do traditional activities together.

My family celebrates Diwali, the festival of lights. One of our traditions is lighting candles.

Most religions have traditions. Traditions are a certain way of thinking or doing something. They are often passed down.

On Palm Sunday, some people fold palm leaves.

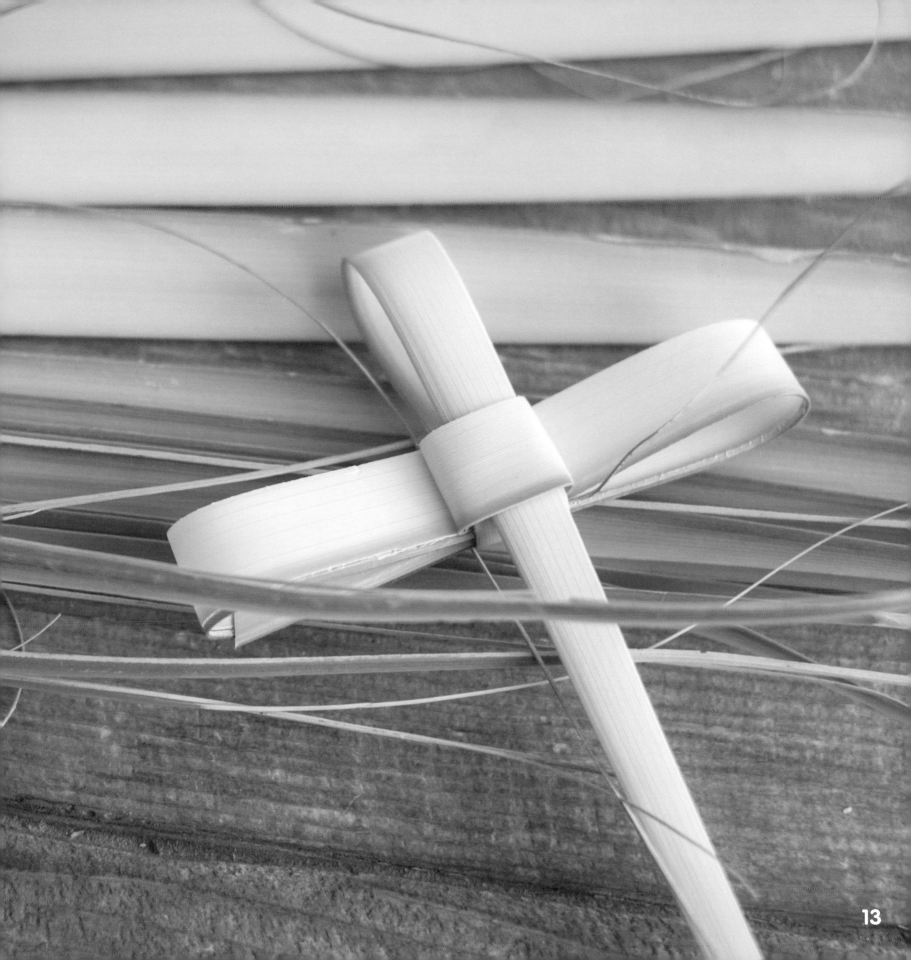

Special foods are an important part of holidays.
Some people start their Eid al-Fitr feast with a date.

This food is part of a Passover celebration.

I love to eat matzah on Passover.

Music is important to a lot of religions. Bhajans are special songs for people who practice Hinduism.

I love to sing with my family and friends.

17

People have many different beliefs. The most important thing is that we show respect and kindness to one another.

Each person's beliefs are important.

Proud to Be Me!

Find a sheet of paper and something to draw with. Draw a picture of how you practice your religion or values.

20

We value
friendship!

Glossary

belief: an idea that a person or community considers to be true

celebration: an event held for a special occasion, like a birthday or a holiday

holiday: an important cultural or religious event

respect: a feeling that someone or something is important and should be treated that way

tradition: a way of thinking or doing something that people have done for a long time

Learn More

Bullard, Lisa. *A Special Invitation: All Kinds of Religions.* Minneapolis: Lerner Publications, 2022.

Ganeri, Anita. *All Kinds of Beliefs*. New York: Crabtree, 2020.

Yuksel, M. O. *In My Mosque*. New York: Harper, 2021.

Index

Photo Acknowledgments

Image credits: GagliardiPhotography/Shutterstock.com, p. 4 (top); Rawpixel.com/Shutterstock.com, p. 4 (bottom left); Golden Pixels LLC/Shutterstock.com, p. 4 (bottom right); Meinzahn/iStock/Getty Images, p. 6 (top); Mint Images/Getty Images, p. 6 (bottom left); Ray Tan/iStock/Getty Images, p. 6 (bottom right); Nobutoshi Akao/Moment via Getty Images, p. 7; IndiaPix/IndiaPicture/Getty Images, p. 8 (top); Adam Berry/Alamy Stock Photo, p. 8 (bottom); Jasmin Merdan/Moment/Getty Images, p. 9; photosindia/Getty Images, p. 10; Tetra Images/Getty Images, p. 13; Elena Eryomenko/Shutterstock.com, p. 14; New Africa/Shutterstock.com, p. 15; Christophe Boisvieux/The Image Bank/Getty Images, p. 16; Chris Pancewicz/Alamy Stock Photo, p. 17; FatCamera/E+/Getty Images, p. 18 (top); Ariel Skelley/DigitalVision/Getty Images, p. 18 (bottom left); kali9/E+/Getty Images, p. 18 (bottom right); Inna Kirkorova/Shutterstock.com, p. 20.

Cover: Mayur Kakade/Moment/Getty Images (top); Rawpixel.com/Shutterstock.com (middle); Drazen Zigic/Shutterstock.com (bottom).

Content consultant credit: Dr. Yvonne Chireau

Lerner Publications Company
An imprint of Lerner Publishing Group, Inc.
241 First Avenue North
Minneapolis, MN 55401 USA

For reading levels and more information, look up this title at www.lernerbooks.com.

Main body text set in Mikado. Typeface provided by HVD.

Designer: Laura Otto Rinne

Library of Congress Cataloging-in-Publication Data

Names: Peterson, Christy, author.
Title: Many ways to believe / Christy Peterson.
Description: Minneapolis: Lerner Publications, [2023] | Series: Sesame Street celebrating you and me | Includes bibliographical references and index. | Audience: Ages 4–8 | Audience: Grades K–1 | Summary: "Many people follow a religion and many people do not. We can respect people and their values. Learn with friends from Sesame Street about religions, holidays, special places, showing respect, and much more"—Provided by publisher.
Identifiers: LCCN 2021051309 (print) | LCCN 2021051310 (ebook) | ISBN 9781728456218 (lib. bdg.) | ISBN 9781728463766 (pbk.) | ISBN 9781728462097 (eb pdf)
Subjects: LCSH: Religion—Juvenile literature. | Religions—Juvenile literature.
Classification: LCC BL48 .P425 2023 (print) | LCC BL48 (ebook) | DDC 200—dc23/eng/20211217

LC record available at https://lccn.loc.gov/2021051309
LC ebook record available at https://lccn.loc.gov/2021051310

Manufactured in the United States of America
1-50691-50110-3/22/2022